P9-BHR-953

One Life. 6 Words. What's Yours?

One Life. 6 Words. What's Yours?

Six-Word Memoirs
From SMITH Magazine

Edited by
Rachel Fershleiser *and* Larry Smith

Harper
Press

HarperPress
An imprint of HarperCollinsPublishers
77–85 Fulham Palace Road
Hammersmith, London W6 8JB
www.harpercollins.co.uk

Visit our authors' blog: www.fifthestate.co.uk

The editors would like to thank SMITH Magazine cofounder Tim Barkow, who was there from word one; Twitter, which helped spread the word fast and far; and the thousands of brilliant memoirists who shared the words in the first place.

All photographs and illustrations are courtesy of the contributors unless otherwise noted.

Photograph on page ii courtesy of Justin Dodd.

First published in Great Britain by HarperPress in 2008

1

A catalogue record for this book
is available from the British Library

ISBN 978-0-00-728470-2

Typeset in:
DIN Schrift, Futura, Granjon, Helvetica Neue, Interstate, LinotypeTypo American, Minion, Rotis Sans, Rotis Serif, Stempel Garamond & Trade Gothic

Printed and bound in Great Britain by Clays Ltd, St Ives plc

Mixed Sources

Product group from well-managed
forests and other controlled sources
www.fsc.org   Cert no. SW-COC-1806
© 1996 Forest Stewardship Council

FSC is a non-profit international organisation established to promote the responsible management of the world's forests. Products carrying the FSC label are independently certified to assure consumers that they come from forests that are managed to meet the social, economic and ecological needs of present or future generations.

Find out more about HarperCollins and the environment at
www.harpercollins.co.uk/green

Introduction

LEGEND HAS IT THAT ERNEST HEMINGWAY WAS ONCE challenged to write a story in six words. Papa came back swinging with, "For sale: baby shoes, never worn." Some say he called it his best work. Others dismiss the anecdote as a literary folktale. Either way, the six-word story was born, and it's been popping around the writing world for years.

Launched online in 2006, SMITH Magazine celebrates personal storytelling and the ways in which technology has fueled storytelling's growth and infinite possibilities. We like to be both populist and aspirational, blurring the line between professional and amateur. So in November 2006, while thousands of people were cranking out tens of thousands of words during annual National Novel Writing Month, SMITH decided to lower the bar. We gave Hemingway's form a new, personal twist: What would a six-word memoir look like?

We asked our friends; they liked the idea. We ran it by memoirists we admire; they loved the challenge. We shared it with the tech communication wizards at Twitter.com; they wanted to team up to deliver a six-worder a day, free to anyone with a cell phone and a love of stories. With those pieces in place, we invited our readers to submit their short, short life stories for a contest—a battle of brevity.

Soon, six-word wonders were zipping across the Net—from laptops to SMITH, from Twitter to cell phones, from writers to their blogs, from readers to one another. And before we knew it, submissions were coming in by the thousands. Folks from all over the world sent in their sublime frustrations (**"One tooth, one cavity, life's cruel"**) and inspired aspirations (**"Business school? Bah! Pop music? Hurrah!"**), their divine wisdom (**"Savior complex makes for many disappointments"**), and deepest inner secrets ("I like big butts, can't lie"). And while most of the memoirs were penned by writers who have not been published (until now), others came from household names—from Aimee Mann (whose six is like a short, sweet song) to Mario Batali (who sent a generous half dozen to our table) to Joan Rivers (as outrageous and wonderful as you'd imagine).

We were most struck by the openness of the memoirists—and by their desire to share even more of their lives with perfect strangers. People sent us pictures of the adorable children they'd just admitted, in six words, they regretted having. One woman wrote us a letter detailing the infertility developments that had rendered her hopeful memoir obsolete. "Whole lifetimes happen in people's lives every day," she wrote, "so I suspect many memoirists write what's true at the time only to find their lives drastically different a short distance in the future."

The enthused author of "Hockey is not just for boys" sent in a photo essay of chicks with sticks, plus the skate-blade sharpening machine of which she's grown so fond. An artist in San Francisco followed up his book illustration with a comic strip about Anna Nicole Smith. We received photos of deceased wives in bridal gowns, of the tiny headstones of babies lost. An accountant in Florida requested a snail-mail address; soon a packet of miniature origami animals arrived at our office.

Others were rising to the occasion in ways we hadn't expected. We heard that teachers were assigning six-word memoirs to their students; that families were trading six-word memoirs across their dinner tables; that pet fanatics were writing them for their dogs.

We became as obsessed as our own memoirists. Wisdom started to appear everywhere in six-word increments. When a hand dryer in a public restroom bore the graffiti "love me or leave me alone," we took it as a six-word sign from above. We had whole conversations while counting on our fingers (and one thumb) for six-word legitimacy. We found ourselves debating the validity of hyphens over dinner and drinks. (Just how many words is "three-legged cat"?)

The fruit of this amazing response? You're holding it in your hands.

One of the delights of reading six-word memoirs is imagining the writer behind those few carefully chosen words. Despite the well-documented dangers of assumption, we were surprised to learn how many of the real-life writers were nothing like we expected.

The bittersweet **"Cursed with cancer. Blessed with friends"** came not from a wise, optimistic grandmother, but a nine-year-old thyroid-cancer survivor. The brave girl's mother wrote to say that her daughter had sat alone at the computer for hours selecting her words, and then checked SMITH each day, hoping to see her name on the screen. The poignant **"I still make coffee for two"** didn't come from the shaky hand of an elderly widower, but a recently dumped twenty-seven-year-old dude with a fondness for caffeine. After months of reading six-word memoirs barely noticing the writer's name, sometimes we were delighted by words seven and eight. After all, could you ask for a better life story from Deepak Chopra's son than **"Soul'd out so I could prophet"**?

This book is a glorious mishmash of these and myriad other voices; it's a thousand little windows into humanity—six words at a time. Whether the results are shocking, strange, silly, or sad, we hope you'll agree that they are always entertaining, often inspiring, and totally addictive.

In the autobiographical spirit of SMITH Magazine, the photos and illustrations that appear here arrived from the writers themselves. To see hundreds of images we didn't have room for, plus new memoirs every day, go to **www.sixword-memoir.com**. While you're there, you just might be struck by an overwhelming desire to supply a six-word memoir of your own. And why wouldn't you: Everyone has a story—what's yours?

The editors of SMITH Magazine
September 2007
New York, NY

One Life. 6 Words. What's Yours?

After Harvard, had
baby with crackhead.

Robin Templeton

Seventy years, few tears, hairy ears.

Bill Querengesser

Watching quietly from
every door frame.

Nicole Resseguie

Catholic school backfired.
Sin is in!

Nikki Beland

Savior complex makes for
many disappointments.

Alanna Schubach

Nobody cared, then they did.
Why?

Chuck Klosterman

Some cross-eyed kid,
forgotten then found.

Diana Welch

She said she was negative.
Damn.

Ryan McRae

Born in the desert,
still thirsty.

Georgene Nunn

A sake mom, not soccer mom.

Shawna Hausman

I asked.

They answered.

I wrote.

Sebastian Junger

No future, no past. Not lost.

Matt Brensilver

Extremely responsible, secretly longed for spontaneity.

Sabra Jennings

`Joined Army. Came out.`
`Got booted.`

Johan Baumeister

Almost a victim of my family.

Chuck Sangster

The psychic said I'd be richer.

Elizabeth Bernstein

Grumpy old soundman
needs love, too.

Lennie Rosengard

Mom died, Dad screwed us over.

Lesley Kysely

**Painful nerd kid,
happy nerd adult.**

Linda Williamson

Write about sex,
learn about love.

Martha Garvey

Stole wife. Lost friends.
Now happy.

Po Bronson

Fourteen years old,
story still untold.

David Gidwani

One long train ride to darkness.

Wayne Colodny

Wolf! She cried.
No one listened.

May Lee

I'm my mother and I'm fine.

K. Bertrand

All day I dream about sex.

Guro Tupchileshtoff

I still make coffee for two.

Zak Nelson

I like girls. Girls like boys.

Andrea Dela Cruz

Never should have bought
that ring.

Paul Bellows

Sold belongings.
Became Itinerant Poetry Librarian.

Sara Wingate Gray

Adventures, joys, love
beyond my desserts.

Max Hastings

Stranded by ten-
thousand-mile crush.

Will Cockrell

Wasted time regretted
so life reinvented.

Vicky Oppus

College was fun.
Damn student loans.

Randy Boland

Semicolons;
I use them to excess.

Iris Page

Womb. Bloom. Groom.
Gloom. Rheum. Tomb.

Blake Morrison

Time heals all wounds? Not quite.

Jonathan Miles

Oldest of five. Four degrees. Broke.

Kaitlin Walsh

Made a mess. Cleaned it up.

Amy Anderson

A crush on Susan Sarandon.
Unrequited.

Willy Edge

Says deaf boyfriend:
you're too quiet.

Anna Jane Grossman

Alive 38 years, feels like 83.

Bryan Lowry

My family is overflowing with therapists.

Shaina Feinberg

Boy, if I had a hammer.

Tim Barkow

We still don't hear a single.

Adam Schlesinger

Lost my hair,
kept my cool.

Alison Michell

Years in the closet.
Why? Why?

Michael Callahan

Docens liberos veritatem
   vitam mihi docet.

Michael Farmer

I did ask to live backwards.

Helen Glynn

Forest peace, sharing vision,
always optimistic.

Dr. Jane Goodall

Bespectacled, besneakered,
read and ran around.

Rachel Fershleiser

Supported the sublime
with uncurbed enthusiasm.

Jeff Newelt

Followed white rabbit.
Became black sheep.

Gabrielle Maconi

Middle of seven
made me me.

Susan Sinnott

The woman formerly
known as Marissa.

Mimi Ghez

Followed yellow brick road.
Disappointment ensued.

Kelsey Ochs

I do not intend to mellow.

Jeffrey Archer

Born free, but lost my country.

Ted O'Brien

Recent doctorate means overeducated
and underemployed.

Philip Sternberg

Taking a lifetime to grow up.

Mirona Iliescu

Living for Jesus because
earth sucks.

Johnny Johnson

Bad brakes
discovered
at high speed.

Paul Schultz

Danced in
Fields of Infinite
Possibilities.

Deepak Chopra

Soul'd out so
I could prophet.

Gotham Chopra

Strange name.
  Transparent shame.
Instant fame.

Bumble Ward

In the office. It smells here.

Meera Parthasarathy

I am trying, in every regard.

Lionel Shriver

Birth, childhood,
  adolescence, adolescence,
  adolescence, adolescence. . .

Jim Gladstone

Happiest when ignoring
huge financial debt.

Ayanna Bryan

© 2007 K. KNIGHT FOR SMITH MAG

Keith Knight

Not pretty enough
so now unemployed.

Stacey Smith

I threw away my
teddy bear.

Margot Loren

Mistakes were made,
but smarter now.

Christine Triano

**Likes everything too
much to choose.**

Rachel Lindenthal

Curly haired sad kid chose fun.

Stacy Abramson

Now I blog and drink wine.

Peter Bartlett

Egomaniac with inferiority
complex defies odds.

Lynne Vittorio

I thought I was someone else.

Tysa Goodrich

Dancing for now,
one day farming.

Eleanor Carpenter

Amazing grace:
born naked, clothed others.

Mark Budman

Followed rules,
    not dreams.
        Never again.

Margaret Hellerstein

    My baby's name
was Sydney Jane.

Margot Bertoni

Love the men.
Hate the commitment.

Lindsay Filz

I grew and grew and
    grew.

Randy Newcomer

Starving artist.
Lucky break.
Life downhill.

Will Samson

My spiritual path
is 100 proof.

John House

I believe in life
before death.

Jonathan Dimbleby

Yes to every date, met mate.

Maria Dahvana Headley

The Hustle: turn
champion into sucker.

Amarillo Slim

I was born some assembly required.

Eric Jordan

I drank too much last night.

Meg McIntyre

Study mathematics.
Marry slut. Sum bad.

Dan Robinson

Took scenic route,
got in late.

Will Blythe

Raised Jehovah's Witness.
Excommunicated at 22.

Kyria Abrahams

I like big butts,

can't lie.

Dave Russ

I hope to outlive my regrets.

Bob Logan

I'm enjoying

downward

even this

dance.

Colum McCann

My first

    proper girlfriend:

        Emily Brontë.

Toby Litt

All night phone calls
complete me.

Harry Manning

Tragic childhood can
lead to wisdom.

Kristin Ahlemeier-Olfe

Sweet wife,
    good sons – I'm rich.

Roger Waggener

Barrister, barista,
what's the diff, Mom?

Abigail Moorhouse

Mom, Dad. Daphne, Owen. Who's next?

Sean Wilsey

Which comes first:
tequila or accident?

Penelope Whitney

Doing more for less is life.

Rondell Conway

Cried. Defied, Denied. Sighed.
Died. Reapplied.

Josh Gosfield

A sundress will solve
life's woes.

Kristen Grimm

I recognize red flags
faster, now.

Barbara Burri

I sucked even the lobster legs.

Rufus Griscom

Anything's possible with
an extension cord.

billySIRR

In and out
of hot water.

Piper Kerman

Life has gone to the dogs.

Ted Rheingold

Born in the U.S.; happy elsewhere.

Julia Napier

Nothing profound,
I just sat around.

Daniel Rosenburg

Found true love,
married someone else.

Bjorn Stromberg

Others left early:
he continued looking.

Anthony Swofford

Shy Jersey kid,
overcompensating ever since.

Ariel Kaminer

Dad died, mom crazy, me, too.

Moby

**Being a
monk stunk.
Better gay.**

Bob Redman

Quiet guy; please pay closer attention.

Jonathan Lesser

Oklahoma girl meets world.
Regrets it.

Gretchen Wahl

Life was but a dream,
merrily.

Paul W. Morris

Happiness is a warm salami sandwich.

Stanley Bing

Creative and destructive
in many ways.

Meghan DeRoma

I sell hamburgers, and french fries.

Richard Maurer

Coffee junkie journalist
seeks trendy nerd.

Jackie Olson

Fight. like. hell.
for. the. living.

Susie Bright

On her birthday,
my life began.

Lisa Parrack

The shit invariably hits the fan.

Ashleea Nielsen

Blogging is easy.
Writing is hard.

Jennifer Shreve

Quit Uni, have baby, now bored.

Samantha Ng

I fell in love
with Charlie.

Kristine Allouchery

And he nerded
as never before.

Jon Thysell

Single typist:
laugh till I cry.

A. L. Kennedy

Fix a toilet,
get paid crap.

Jennifer James

Tow truck drivers
are my psychiatrists.

Joanne McNeil

Should have
used condom
that time.

Rob Bigelow

Macular
degeneration.
Didn't see
that coming.

Ian Gould

Fifty years so far.
Happened fast.

Mark Michaelson

**Atheist
plus Methodist
make
Jewish children.**

Richard Michelson

Infinite calm beset with
emotional architecture.

DJ Spooky

`Won the fight;`
`lost the girl.`

Jim O'Grady

Near death experiences
are my forte.

Anna Mauser-Martinez

Illustration by Josh Neufeld

Fight, work, persevere —
gain slight notoriety.

Harvey Pekar

Lived in moment until moment sucked.

Janine Goss

She said nothing could go wrong.

Derek Powazek

Laughing until I pee my pants.

Carolyn Waller

Go find your father; my life.

Adam Danielson

Life goal:
Maximum results, minimal effort.

Phil Kahn

It was all too brief.

Rudolph Delson

Quite undecided, yet hopefully
unsatisfied, generally.

Daniel Gumbiner

Took a spectacle, made it sport.

Dana White

Slightly psychotic, in a good way.

Patricia Neelty

She walked barefoot
in wet cement.

Michelle Pinchev

As a child, nomadic. Now static.

Kristin Gotski

Should have lived more, written less.

John Banville

Found true love after
nine months.

Jody Smith

Hillbilly does right
by his teeth.

Jason Snyder

No words can describe my life.

John Baldridge

Afraid of everything.
Did it anyway.

Ayse Erginer

On the playground, alone.
1970, today.

Charles Warren

I wrote it all down somewhere.

Ben Greenman

**Inside suburban mom
beats urban heart.**

Julie Goss

Missed Halley's Comet.
Miss virginity too.

Yoz Grahame

Not a good Christian,
but trying.

Alexander Tsai

Paid cash and never
stopped running.

David Marston

Lost and found, rescued by dog.

Gail Reilly

Afraid of becoming
like my mother.

Jocelyn Pearce

Goodbye Fat Kim: I now live.

Kim Kaufman

Two boys, my life,
conquering autism.

Michelle DePasquale

Pleased
I never did page 3.

Katrina Naomi

I could
never get anything
quite right.

Harry Enfield

Stop
Bothering
Me.
Trying to work.

Paul Whitehouse

What the hell.
Might as well.

Nancy London

Old age is not all bad.

Anna Massey

Sometimes I'm crazy,
sometimes I'm sane.

Bella Von Phul

Can't tonight,
watching *Law & Order*.

Rory Evans

Musician gone bad. Darn law school!

Stephen Adams

I take photographs. I see life.

Daniel James

Hippie parents.
Early independence.
Surprising success.

Darci Groves

My life's a bunch of almosts.

Shari Bonnin

Struggled with how
the mind works.

Steven Pinker

It's not you. It's me. Honest.

Allison Glock

Brought it to a boil, often.

Mario Batali

Scribbling twit dreaming
lit every minute.

Jamie Grove

Thought I would have
more impact.

Kevin Clark

This is aggression in pink, Mom.

Nicole Tourtelot

Graduated May.
2I June.
Married July.

Amara Rockar

Oh, to have just one puff!

Suhana Selamat

**Bad reputation,
such a good girl.**

Erin Oldroyd

Mom left. Returned!
Left. Reconciliation! Cancer.

Kelly Streit

Laughing intellectual
ronin danced,
unlearning lies.

Tom Buckner

At the end of normal street.

Tracey Morgan

Found great happiness
in insignificant details.

Alisdair McDiarmid

Spent life looking
for dead people.

Melody Lassalle

Forty Five.
Never Married.
Oh poo.

Sonia Oney

Enjoying my fuck ups too much.

Susan Crippin

My reach always exceeds my grasp.

Ray Garraud

Marked time till 55,
reborn thereafter.

Doug Fraser

The race is not **to** the **swift** nor **the** battle **to** the **strong** neither **yet** bread **to** the **wise** nor **yet** riches **to** men **of** understanding **nor** yet **favour** to men of **skill** but **that** time **and** chance **happen** to **them** all! Ha!

D.B.C. Pierre

Four children in four decades;
whew!

Loretta Serrano

An unusual turn
of gender
circumstances.

Dragana Varadinac

Hiding in apartment knitting
against depression.

Laurie White

She kissed me and said yes!

Ricardo Saramago

Dabbler in much, expert in none.

Joan Cady

Once wed,
     twice loved,
          past prime.

Betty Black

My life is full of action.

Hannah Maconodie

Always dreamt of kissing pretty girls.

Jessica Furey

I lost god. I found myself.

Joe Kimmel

Everyone who loved me is dead.

Ellen Fanning

Caring for parents • life is circular •

Timothy McGrath

It was embarrassing,
so don't ask.

Alex Lindquist

Verbal hemophilia.
Why can't I clot?

Scott Mebus

Time to start over again,
again.

Dan Petronelli

Always even keel
except when sailing.

Maryann Pirrotta

Still lost on road less traveled.

Joe Quesada

Over fifty, still a Boy Scout!

Jerry Richstein

The car accident
changed my life.

Kristin Stanefski

Said goodbye,
hasn't shut up since.

Michael Collins

Burned my bridges
and my britches.

Dave Zablocki

See you tomorrow, small
wars permitting

Christina Lamb

Older now, I draw myself better.

Peter Arkle

Batteries are cheap.
  Who needs men?

Rebecca McLenna

Clueless meets Ophelia,
  without the suicide.

Larisa Ballinger

My boyfriend is blonder than me.

Sophie Reynolds

Had ambition;
  had kids;
    bloomed late.

Bronia Kita

Artsy married Fartsy,
has two kids.

Mary Organ

Anything possible – but I was tired.

Cheryl Family

I ate, drank, and was hairy.

Yianni Varonis

Girlfriend is pregnant, my husband said.

Shonna MacDonald

I am awfully bored at work.

Chris Ponchak

Learned reading, writing, forgot arithmetic.

Elizabeth Gruner

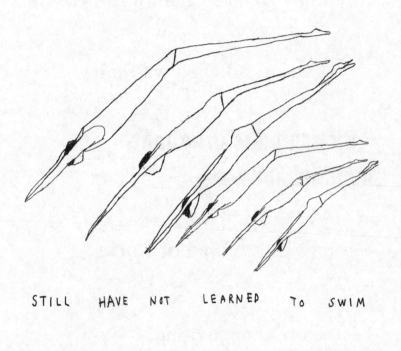

STILL HAVE NOT LEARNED TO SWIM

Lauren Redniss

Trying to medicate my redneck past.

Garrett Sparks

Lucky in love,
   unlucky in metabolism.

Leah Weathersby

I live the perfect
imperfect life.

Paul Lore

Ate caterpillars.
   Still won't grow up.

Chris Jackson

Wannabe heroine but
   just Plain Jane.

Tanya Holland

Civil servant answers phone after five.

Jason Prince

Glass half full;
pockets half empty.

Marina Guthrie

We undercover agents need
mental toughness.

Joe Pistone

Rebel librarian on
sabbatical from boys.

Heather Meagher

Arthur-ectomy taking years!
Beware: wed cautiously.

Natalie Windsor

Woman Seeks Men –
High Pain Threshold.

Yin Shih

No Wife.
No Kids.
No Problems.

Rip Riley

You are all in my imagination.

Becky Weinberg

School geek married a
luscious cheerleader.

Christopher Clukey

I couldn't protect me
from myself.

Patrick Eleey

Eat mutate aura amateur auteur true.

Jonathan Lethem

Aspiring lady pirate,
disillusioned, sells boat.

Diana White

Dad died. Mum died. I'm next.

Jim Crace

Married for money.
Divorced for love.

Rosie Abraham

**My life
is a beautiful accident.**

J. D. Tenuta

Thank God I lived
through Vietnam.

Captain John Irving

Meat and potatoes man
  goes vegetarian.

Perette Lawrence

  Smart, tall, independent
woman. Men scarce.

Annie Schmidt

I was and now I'm not.

Gayla Buyukas

Oh sweet nectar of life, coffee.

Daniel Axenty

Young, skinny, ridiculed.
  Old, skinny, envied.

Phil Sweet

No shit I'm critical –
  you're flawed.

Elizabeth Koch

It's pretty high. You go first.

Alan Eagle

One tooth,
   one cavity,
      life's cruel.

John Bettencourt

In a Manolo world, I'm Keds.

Colleen Cook

Lonely gay
    hates work,
       loves play.

Ray Ivey

Wasn't noticed
so I painted trains.

Mare 139

Mind says no, heart says yes.

Will Young

Running away:
best decision I made.

Stephen Elliott

I served my debt to society.

Michael Frisch

Scarred by 9/11;
helped by penguins.

Audrey Blackburn

Fleeting nights, cloudy mornings,
coffee's ablution.

Heath Hardin

When she proposed, I said yes.

Josh Neufeld

Black Latina. Slave ship
stopped everywhere.

Veronica Chambers

My heart is deaf,
head dumb.

David Matthews

**My first concert: Zappa.
Explains everything.**

Janet Tashjian

Nobody knows how
I have suffered.

Tim Hall

A brilliant pen but invisible ink.

Christina Samuel

**Wandering imagination opens
doors to paradise.**

Rebecca Perlstein

**After eighteen years,
sold my book.**

Susan Runholt

Too many lovers –
too little time.

Joel Kincaid

Six words not enough for a

Laura Hillenbrand

Couldn't
cope so I wrote
songs.

Aimee Mann

Happy childhood found
again in teaching.

Matthew Friday

Angry guy gets law
license, sues.

Bryan Gates

Long lost girl
recently found, unharmed.

Tracy Bishop

Gave commencement address,
became sex columnist.

Amy Sohn

3,000 miles away from the truth.

Michael Slenske

Mormon economist marries
feminist. Worlds collide.

Michael McBride

Mormon feminist loves
husband, hates patriarchy.

Caroline Kline

**Followed dim shapes through
narcotic haze.**

John Law

Mom, Dad have dementia. Got gun?

Carol Belding

Born a twin, died a loner.

Heather Thompson

Young optimist:
proven wrong.
Prematurely old.

Buzzy Porter

It was worth it, I think.

Annette Laitinen

Students laughed appreciatively.
The professor relaxed.

Laurie Hensley

Drink because I am a poet.

Maria Essig

People always pronounce
my name incorrectly.

Linnea Jimison

**Dorothy Gale had
the right idea.**

Pamela Vissing

Dropped out, got out,
lucked out.

Ben Kweller

I was never the pretty one.

Joan Nesbit Mabe

Born at 23,
childhood doesn't count.

Krissy Karol

Perpetual work in progress, need editor.

Sherry Fuqua-Gilson

**She loves
(I write)
Her life.**

Miranda Seymour

I was
the only
planned sibling.

Mary Sebas

Age grows,
I've finally
accepted me.

Kate Mammolito

Paralyzed
at fifty, life
still nifty.

Gib Henderson

Snuggling, setups.
  These are my specialties.

Laura Cooper

**Was big boy,
now little man.**

Chris Cooper

Two habitats.

Cornwall.

Scotland.

Lucky me.

Rosamunde Pilcher

Ex-con making good
on lifestyle promise.

Doug Houston

Canoe guide, only got lost once.

Taylor Stump

Aging late bloomer
    yearns for do-over.

Sydney Zvara

American backbone,
Arab marrow,
much trouble.

Rabih Alameddine

Memory was my drug
of choice.

Pea Hicks

Liars, hysterectomy *didn't* improve sex life!

Joan Rivers

Mom, sorry I moved to U.S.

Yuri Fukazawa

Unhappy joke writer
hugs her chihuahua.

Jessica Salmonson

Boys liked her.
She preferred books.

Anneliese Cuttle

Wife died young; on the mend.

Sumit Paul-Choudhury

I'm ten, and have
an attitude.

Tillie Seger

Gay physician designed
life-saving AIDS drugs.

Laurent Fischer

Never lived up to my potential.

Leslie Sterling

My twin died but I survived.

Rebecca Farmer

Tequila. Amnesia. Coincidence?
I think not.

Larry Caraviello

Carbohydrates call my
name every day.

Mary Petersdorf

Never really
finished
anything,
except cake.

Carletta Perkins

Cursed with cancer.
Blessed with friends.

Hannah Davies

Crappy parents killed
my self esteem.

Julie Doherty

Lonely artist turned
waitress in love.

Gretchen Bone

Does my biological mother
cry sometimes?

Steven Schmidt

My life is just like yours.

Matt Stephens

Some collect coins,
I collect diplomas.

Srini Rajagopalan

Bipolar at 12, lithium at 36.

Linda Hatfield-Southern

Inquisitive, excited, surprised and
sometimes wrong.

Jon Snow

If Eliza Doolittle
wore cowboy boots . . .

Dixie Friedman

Ex-wife and contractor
now have house.

Drew Peck

Fifteen years since last professional haircut.

Dave Eggers

Midlife crisis uncovers queer
intellectual's talent.

Donald W. Jacobson

**Fat jolly bearded
origami-folding accountant.**

Gary Mullings

Lucky in everything
else but love.

Eliot Sheridan

`Mixed blood.`
`I am America's future.`

Holly Santiago

I'm just here for the beer.

Alex Vournas

With three cats I'm never unloved.

Cynthia Macdonald

Missing limb, cruel world,
love overcomes.

James Mallon

Divorced twice,
lived happily ever after.

Susan Guyaux

Torrential tryst.
Terrible twins. Tied tubes.

M. Brenner

Can my words have
footnotes, please?

Amy Harbottle

So it goes,
a tad askew.

Michael Dickter

Alas, a farewell to legs. Next!

Allen Rucker

Came, saw, conquered,
had second thoughts.

Harold Ramis

Left a desert for a
wasteland.

James Slone

City streets,
saggy shoes,
and poetry.

Arianna Kandell

The weather is better
up here.

Brad Wieners

Beat death thrice.
Still not religious.

Shan Palmer

Found love.
Got hitched in Vegas.

Jami Brandli

**Baby dyke now raising
two babies.**

Andrea Selch

Stoned. Boned.
Where am I now?

Sherry Levy

New Jersey to California.
Thank God.

Ayelet Waldman

Town car,
  tailored suit,
    dirty nails.

Nicole Blades

Bipolar
secretary
girlfriend mama
hen oddball.

Teressa Fly

Learning to be great
at mediocrity.

Christopher Reiger

Jewfro and glasses,
  laughter and yoga.

Deborah Greene

I fell far from the tree.

Rebecca Stadolnik

Huh. Hmm.

Really?

Jesus! Oy ve.

Ian Sansom

After your jump,
the net appears.

Vincent Lauria

I don't know
but Google
does.

Sorcha Exworthy

I colored
   outside of the lines.

Jacob Thomas

Without me, it is just
aweso.

Chris Madigan

Me: consistently avoiding
death since 1978!

Daniel Fowlkes

I think,
     therefore
I am bald.

Dickie Widjaja

Should not have eaten
those mushrooms.

Emilie Raguso

Wanked furiously. Married. Furious no more.

John Heppolette

Wealthy

woman

escapes

with handsome

mailman.

April Shewan

IBM brat broke back; twins, Mac.

John Hockenberry

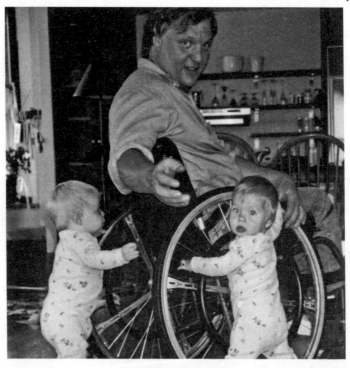

Love annihilated a
thirty-year age difference.

Betsy Smith

Saw, interpreted,
mourned, hoped, then
preached.

Douglas Rushkoff

Even the quietest sounds
make noise.

Paul Boggan

I grew up in a cemetery.

Rachael Hanel

Many hands have kept me afloat.

Nick Flynn

Man of the world = alien immigrant.

Rajat Suri

```
Ran away with
circus; never
returned.
```

Ellia Bisker

I managed not to
destroy anything.

Tucker Frazier

All of my students hate me.

Sharon Fishfeld

Gay white African
emigrates, finds love.

Graham Coppin

The world was enough. I wasn't.

Michel Faber

Buxom songstress
loves love and chocolate.

Angie Arnold

Blade cuts, blood runs,
scars remain.

Heather Hudgins

Did I miss a deadline again?

Bruce McGill

Walking the green mile:
finally free.

Alejandro Echeverra

Redhead woman,
raucous curves,
makes music.

Shannon Russell

Dreamy visions during extended daytime hours

Katherine Streeter

Love drama,
just not my own.

Sam Zalutsky

I wouldn't change it a bit.

Ann Paxton

Saw the world;
now where's home?

Hannah Silverstein

Nose broken, beauty queen
changes profession.

Dan Rubin

Nineteen forty-nine to two
thousand . . . something.

Anne Greer

Blinked! Winked!
I am halfway through!

Vinod Pillai

Arms: full. Life: not so much.

Renee James

Quietly
cultivating my
inner Lynda Carter.

Joanna Sheehan

Many risky mistakes,
very few regrets.

Richard Schnedl

Six kids; life stranger than fiction!

Deborah Carson

He left me for good eventually.

Audrie Lawrence

Liberal at 18.
Conservative by 40.

Pat Ryan

Would you like fries
with that?

Scott Northrup

I won Miss Union
Pier 1952.

Elaine Yonover

**Legs spread,
I withheld my
intelligence.**

Christine Granados

Next time –
better parents, better hair.

Ruth Romano

Bald, Brunette, Blonde,
Grey, White, Bald.

Ann Widdecombe

Traversing Earth together, chasing
elusive answers.

Paul Barber

**Considered life, then death.
Step, repeat.**

Paul Pope

Hockey is not just for boys.

Alexandra Duplin

Artist, disabled.
    Feeling mislabeled.
        Ambitions tabled.

Patrick Dentinger

Fell in love. Married.
Divorced. Repeat.

Lori McLeese

Never liked the taste
of beets.

Michael Pemberton

Underachieving
pleasure punk seeks
constant gratification.

Dennis Elj

Always working on
the next chapter.

Milan Pham

Business school? Bah!
Pop music? Hurrah!

Max Robins

Happy now that I know myself.

Anne Maiwald

Polka-dotted mayhem
and decadent disasters.

Candace Locklear

Beach mama blissfully buoys
burgeoning brood.

Elizabeth Barr

Risked it all;
wasn't quite enough.

Greta Orris

I write because
I can't sleep.

Ben Mezrich

Sperm too potent,
now have triplets.

Renee Schunk

Never fear.
Truffle season is near.

Barry Glassner

Yes, you can edit
this biography.

Jimmy Wales

The best hair, the worst
shpilkes.

Joanna Arkans

Katie180, you make
my heart crazy.

John Patrick Zito

Started

small,

grew,

peaked,

shrunk,

vanished.

George Saunders

My daughter's baby,
   inconvenient and incredible.

Laurie White

   Mom blames musical theater.
   I disagree.

Dan Sigale

**Clothes, wardrobe,
who's to fit them?**

Sophie Whitehurst

Big, little sister,
stuck in middle.

Joanna Lilly

My lover's lover was my friend.

Wendy Jones

Multiple miscarriages.
Cousin will carry baby.

Joanna Brody

Alone at home, cat on lap.

Christopher Goldthwaite

**Poet locked in body
of contractor.**

Marilyn Hencken

And I never did sober up.

Ray Overfield

Three marriages.
Thirteen novels.
Sleep's overrated.

Jane Heller

World backpacking decade
  ends with minivan.

Cindi Hounton

  Educated too much,
lived too little.

Dan Vance

Lapsed Catholic; failed poet;
unpublished prayers.

Marc Sheehan

Twin girls, double dates,
husbands confused.

Naomi Beth Wakan

  Went long on ride
    toward Providence.

Bill Buck

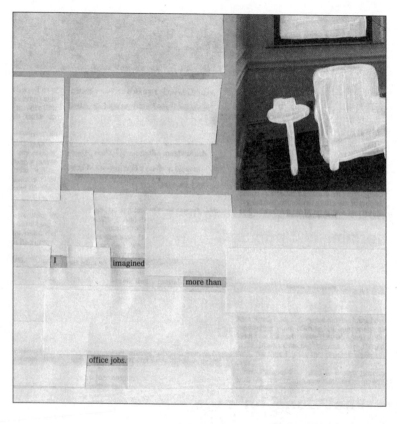

Gretchen Vitamvas

Overjoyed I'm not like
my sister.

Elizabeth DeLamater

Start-Rite Double A;
Cosy-Feet Treble E.

Barbara Trapido

Hope my obituary spells
"debonair" correctly.

Gregg Easterbrook

Just in: boyfriend's gay.
Merry Christmas.

Seshie Hargett

Traded mastheads for
Texas desert sky.

Whitney Joiner

Lucky sperm club
  entrant wins life.

Steve Conlin

Was father, boys died, still sad.

Ronald Zalewski

Tried everything once,
  few things twice.

Ed Zevetski

Baptist Mom. Jewish Dad.
  Atheist. Surprised?

Sara Faith Alterman

**Cheated organizational
systems but never people.**

Ryan Bright

**Asked and
   answered,
   asshole,
   next question.**

Joe Lockhart

**Really, doing fine,
thanks for asking.**

Fuzzy Gerdes

I'd rather be watching a movie.

Lawrence Levi

Never could resist overachieving.

Chris Harris

Her blue eyes
capture the distance.

Sonya Cheuse

Born with glaucoma . . .
fading to black . . .

Susan Giusto

I watched a lot of television.

Adam Hirsch

Oh shit! No way? Yeah
dude.

Ned Vizzini

My angle was an angel
wangle.

Salley Vickers

Five feet, but in
your face.

Toby Berry

Born bald. Grew hair.
Bald again.

A. J. Jacobs

Mistook streetlight for
the moon. Climbed.

Zack Wentz

Boyfriend in bed,
still a lesbian?

Cheryl Burke

I wrote a book about this.

Vittorio Giannini

Wanted to live forever,
died trying.

Syona Luciferina

Hugged some trees,
then burned them.

Tom Price

Happy child, wild teenager,
  adult anarchist.

Dar Wolnik

  Right place, right time,
good lawyer.

Ben Brown

To paraphrase
William Faulkner: I endured.

Don Willmott

To make a long story short . . .

Jace Albao

Famished, I had
seconds . . . and thirds.

Richard Strager

Lazy Renaissance man
settles for dilettantism.

Bradley Lyons

Raised a palimpsest, by many voices.

Saba Cambone

Arab hillbilly goes
to New York.

Alex Cummings

Full life; impossible to

summarize in

Matt Love

Was rebellious teen.
Now raising one.

Michelle Ganon

I have not done it all.

Aaron Knoll

Woke up,
   fell down,
      exited sideways.

Jim Clupper

A new memoir every five years.

Srini Rajagopalan

My second grade teacher
was right.

Janelle Brown

Rather sing than stay to chat.

Keri Willson

Someone had to pay the bills.

David Kuizenga

Didn't fit in then;
still don't.

Bob Fingerman

I love my lady . . .
and bacon.

Jeff Walton

Buried gold long ago.
Can't find.

Maureen Barnes

Later-life serendipity
led to Authorland.

Jeff Schult

A man, a plan, hot damn.

L. Levyne

Revenge is living well,
without you.

Joyce Carol Oates

I forgot I have memory loss.

Mary Hynes

Underachieving . . . but willing to
overcompensate halfheartedly.

Frank J. Lepiane

`A Brooklyn lawyer.`
`Sewer to Sue-er.`

Mo Mann

Outcast.
    Picked last.
        Surprised them all.

Rachel Pine

Country girl seeks,
   finds, abandons city.

Jenny Rose Ryan

What did you say? I'm deaf.

Karen Putz

**Became my mother.
Please shoot me.**

Cynthia Kaplan

Kinetosis, hemihypertrophy, testicular
elephantiasis; pleasureboat recalcitrant.

Roderick Maclean

Explained Hitler, Shakespeare.
Couldn't explain self.

Ron Rosenbaum

If there's more,
I want it.

Alex Hart

It's like forever, only much shorter.

Pete DeVito

God, grant me patience. Right now.

Michael Castleman

Cancer for sure. Still no cure.

Jenn Siebel

Relatively famous parents, very low self-esteem.

Molly Jong-Fast

Pitched. Pitched. Pitched. Wrote. Revised. Revised.

Andrew Adam Newman

Wanted:
    stories heard
        on mother's lap.

Tony Parsons

Woman with man's name
— thanks, parents!

Curtis Sittenfeld

Born lucky, striving to die
worthy.

Julia Carpenter

Tequila made her
clothes fall off.

Susanne Broderick

After Manson,
my life became dull.

Allan Sorensen

I told you I was crazy.

Michaline Babich

Topless dancer.
Circus clown.
Spy.
Writer.

Susan DiRende

Sometimes it rains.
Sometimes I smile.

Peter Hermann

I play dress-up for a living.

Melissa Nicholl

Where the hell are my
keys?

Brady Udall

Bank robber,
prison-humbled,
confesses all.

Joe Loya

Keep dancing and never give up!

Bruce Forsyth

She always wore socks to bed.

Myfanwy Collins

Not as blond as I look.

Ellen Meister

Often alone,
office drone,
feisty crone.

Patty Quickert

Horny small-town boy
becomes writer.

Kevin Sampsell

I closely resemble
my uncle Fred.

Brian Van Nieuwenhoven

Well, I thought
it was funny.

Stephen Colbert

**Strived to become
everything I didn't.**

Richard Tomas

Let's just be friends,
she said.

Mike Pfaffroth

Happenstance, she thought
– but maybe not.

Amelia Allard

Chemistry? No. Law? No.
Motherhood? Yes!

Anneliese Dickman

I died at an early age.

John Coyne

Lived like no tomorrow;
tomorrow came.

C. C. Keiser

Date with geek yields
chip-filled life.

Robin Raskin

I couldn't possibly
fuck him again.

Theodore Bouloukos

Learned everything from words,
pictures, love.

Dan Goldman

This imperfect life,
perfect for perfectionist.

Sarah Gardner

Forgot to say I love her.

Omi Castanar

Can't read all the time.
Bummer.

Rina Bander

I wrote a poem.
Nobody cared.

Joe Heaps Nelson

Put whole self in, shook about.

Melissa Delzio

Not quite what I was planning . . .

Summer Grimes

Mojo
search
resumes,
impossible
flowers
bloom.

Nick Balaban

I inhale battles.
    I exhale victories.

William Heath

Working with what God gave me.

David Schmoyer

Unforgivable, frightening,
unforgettable and life-changing.

Olivia Johncock

Coffee. Coffee.
    Water. Water.
        Wine. Tea.

C. Hunter

Southern queer teacher
plays, sings, laughs.

Amanda Northrup

Same Mistakes.
Over and over again.

Matthew Oransky

Still trying
to impress my dad.

Shoshana Berger

Hatless, shirtless,
shitless. Still, I sang.

Scott Hartwich

Girl loved Jesus. Girl loves boys.

Lindsay Robertson

We were our own
Springer episode.

Michelle Hoogerwerf

. . . exalted philanderer of the
English language . . .

Steven Ekstrom

Laughter and inappropriate
humor since 1985.

Annie Jacobson

I am a cartwheel of mentorship.

Anne Asher

Asked for love.
 Received confusion.
 Waiting.

Irina Kendall

I always suffered
fools fairly well.

Richard Ford

I re-met Lori after 27 years.

Alan Weinkrantz

So devastated, no babies for me.

Jennifer Faulkner

Nobel dad; tough act to follow!

Andreas Wettstein

Me: fully reformed and
halfway happy.

Koren Zailckas

Eat drink
man man
man man.

Michael Musto

The day just kept getting better.

Jeff Cranmer

Met lots of crazy famous people.

Jonathan van Meter

Waited too long to get it.

Rhona Yolkut

Took up photography.
Got the shot.

Keith MacDonald

Strange like cat.
Smart like rat.

Andrew Randall

I answer to the name Mom.

Lynne Chesterton

Girls aren't 6'; I am 5'12.

Marlee Sayen

Born in city that doesn't exist.

Jackie Delamatre

Disco
jeans,
1977:
mine alone
finally.

Susie Park

Fact checker by day,
liar by night.

Andy Young

Weird
quiet
girl fading
from view.

Felicia Sullivan

Four eyes
are better
than two.

Marissa Walsh

Shot my
penis in photo
booth.

Jeffrey Zeldman

After which
he was never sane.

Aleksandar Hemon

Gay
Puerto Rican
in straight clothing.

Ryan Roman

Yes, singing rocks,
but money calls.

Jonathan Cogswell

Almost nothing was
under my control.

Joel Stein

Sold clocks carved
out of soap.

Aaron Fagan

Learned. Forgot. Better off
re-learning anyway.

Brian DeLeeuw

More
broken bones
than broken
hearts.

Evan Rosler

Suburban girl tries to make bad.

Sari Wilson

Wife: one; Degrees: two;
Arrests: seven.

Patrick J. Sauer

Coulda, shoulda, woulda:
a regretful life.

Joe Maida

No pay? Another day? No way.

Heather Steed

Let me in, you
narrative whore.

C. McClosky

**Fearlessness
is the mother of
reinvention.**

Arianna Huffington

It got better after middle age.

Ruth Haworth

God who? Oh, him.
No thanks.

Carin Rhoden

Seeking route,
not sure of destination.

Gary Belsky

Divorced! Thank God
for Internet personals.

Maryrose Wood

Cheese
is the
essence of life.

Mary Lynch

I waste time looking for love.

Sean Gannett

Vietnam Protests.
Equality Protests.
Disability Protests.

Ron Kendricks

My family did not kill me.

David Sampliner

Things happen because
I see holes.

Susan Chi

**Serial missed
connections
end with you.**

Liz Brown-Inz

Born in California.
Then nothing happened.

Mark Harris

Named Hope. How else to be?

Hope Hall

Straight jacket on
the gentle cycle.

Stewart Rudy

Love Brooklyn,
but London still calls.

Sarah Butterworth

Tickle, trample,
come back for more.

Kathryn Waggener

I still secretly read
wedding magazines.

Lestlie Berryhill

Eureka! Margin too small for proof.

Marcus du Sautoy

Eat to live, live to eat.

Tim Toomey

The freaks, they always find me.

Ginger Lime

Wildly crooked,
   unlikely to be straightened.

lê thi diem thúy

Got a pony, broke my arm.

Layne Bell

Should have
learned to count.

David Wheatley

dam smart
never lerned to
spel.

Rachel Ehrlich

My ancestors were
   accented cow herders.

Nina Moog

**Filled blank spaces with
ambitious endeavors.**

Adam Schachner

`Gin joints. Love affairs. No relation.`

Dean Ellis

I traveled each
and every highway.

Sebastian Buhai

Widowed. Forging reluctantly
   forward with faith.

TerriAnn Ferren

Still a very bad Mormon. Yay!

Marsha Brown

This Tolstoy gets
no Oprah promotion.

Victor Pelevin

Political stance makes
my family crazy.

Steve Collins

Once was blind.
Now I see.

David Hansen

Good things happen
to bad people.

Michael Malice

Secret of life:

marry an Italian.

Nora Ephron

Slightly flabby,
    slightly fabulous,
        trying hard.

Amy Friedman

Palindromic novels fall apart halfway through.

Chuck Clark

Saw clearly after blind date. Marriage!

Saralee Rosenberg

Thank god the suicide attempt failed.

Rhett Miller

Made labor-saving software:
    thousands unemployed.

George Girton

I hear nothing and see everyone.

Eunice Chang

Secretly, I dream of

my ex-boyfriend.

Rosally Sapla

Unfortunately,
there was no other way.

Atom Robinson

A daydream, or so it seemed.

Eva Meszaros

She danced, and
did little else.

Sarah Cost

Came out.
Went in.
Came out.

Earl Adams

Only black girl.
Fierce woman now.

Courtney Kemp Agboh

My wife made me do it.

Jeffrey Yamaguchi

Took breath.
Took ill.
Took notes.

Hilary Mantel

birth
bris
bed
bath
and
beyond

Barry Blitt

Like an angel. The fallen kind.

Rick Bragg

Full of tequila and bad ideas.

Buck Johnston

Lived in America.
Came back different.

Nigel French

Lehmann-Haupt, yeah;
not that one.

Rachel Lehmann-Haupt

Expected prime rib;
ended with hamburger.

Bernard Lam

Drew on walls, creative for life.

DeAnna Sandoval

**Unborn baby,
dancing belly,
arriving soon.**

Tami Piccione

Too soon, too late, not enough.

Suzy Parsons

Committed voluntarily,
until trying to leave.

Michael Holland

When all else
fails, start running.

Dean Karnazes

Carnivore and herbivore birth
magical omnivore.

Morgan Spurlock

Never going to
have a dog.

Lily Redman

Asked to quiet down; spoke louder.

Wendy Lee

My computer screen tells it all.

James Browne

Indelibly tenacious,
I read and breed.

Shawna Lisk-Sprester

My next guest is Jesus Christ.

Michael Parkinson

Don't marry a lawyer, be one.

Deborah Schneider

Still waiting for you to ask.

Alice Massey

Ex-addict now addicted
to book deals.

Susan Shapiro

**When talk matters,
make it count.**

Phil Liggett

Love New York;
Hate Self. (Equally.)

David Rakoff

My penultimate act is to imbibe.

Alex Twersky

Mmm, tea.
So stereotypical.
Rule Britannia!

Paul O'Brien

Arty dad, rocker mom,
crazy childhood.

Summer Pierre

Ordering soup for two, for one.

Dan Silverman

Still here despite
logic and likelihood.

Elisha Marshall

She read too much . . .
   into everything.

Jessica Reed

Father, son, both hit by cars.

Gordon Hurd

**Women's magazine
employee now
misogynist novelist.**

Stephanie Lessing

I didn't skateboard
nearly often enough.

Kevin Wilkins

Internet famous,
for what that's worth.

Ron Hogan

Sometimes at night I lay lonely.

Mark Jaynes

Deported once,
legal now – Green Card.

Michael Kaminer

I didn't walk off a roof.

Tobin Levy

Say no now,
I now know.

Steve Woodruff

Left house one day
for cigarettes.

Sheila Ryan

What?

Lemony Snicket?

Lemony Snicket?

What?

Daniel Handler

Made some good choices,
    got lucky.

Matthew Kett

```
Jew-born.
Yeshiva-educated.
Date goyim.
```

Abby Ellin

```
Yorkshire, Surrey,
Hampshire, Isle of
Wight.
```

Alan Titchmarsh

Pay attention to me!
Go away.

Kathy Rogers

**Big hair,
     big heart,
          big hurry.**

Larry Smith

Melancholy marvel at how
everything connects.

Lawrence Weschler

Climbing, porn, crack, science.
Still bored.

Lenny Oliker

I'm the
   fine print;
      read closely.

Kristina Grish

Ran
east,
ran
west,
ran
late.

Susie Smith

Most Turkish Kurd, most Kurdish Turk.

Yasar Kemal

Tall, dark, handsome:
Single, content,
uncommunicative.

Mark Grace

Do as say,
not as did.

Emily Gordon

Good, evil use the
same font.

Arthur Harris

Never a bridesmaid;
always a bride.

Anne Allisoni

I fell out of the nest.

Jason Logan

More than yesterday,
less than tomorrow.

Nichiren Nahuel Palombo

**I don't nibble. I bite.
Hard.**

Matthew Torres

Open road, no map.
Great Scenery.

Tom Gabbay

Maybe you had to be there.

Roy Blount Jr.

Right brain working
left brain job.

Dave Terry

Life behind a microphone
gets lonely.

Crystal Kash

**Spent longing for
the seventh word.**

Ron Bel Bruno

Five continents down; two to go.

Virginia Graham

Affection. Erection.
No protection.
Injection. Infection.

Colleen Zachary

Speaks mind especially when losing it.

Ellis Reid

He knew her bruises would fade.

Colin Stanton

Indeterminate. Not enough data for conclusion.

Ian Grant

I got herpes, in my pants.

Daniel Moyer

Hid for a while.
Not anymore.

Ginger Voight

I
came,
I saw,
I concurred.

Cris Anitsirhc

Afraid of mirrors,
too many marshmallows.

Lihi Lasslo

Bought
American
Dream.
More like
nightmare.

Harry McCoy

I was concerned
about my obituary.

James Dunn

Born red closet reborn SF queer.

David Boyer

Youngest of four girls
turns fifty.

Judi Kolenda

Saw the sky and
started walking.

Mark Sundeen

Learned eventually, Billy Crystal, not Salinger.

Ben Kaplan

Once born,
now old, soon gone.

Andre Vandal

We were married in the snow.

Polly and Andrew McLean

Photograph by Sean Graff

My life, in Mexico, is strange.

Cosima Rose

Awkward girl takes chances.
Fun ensues.

Charlotte Riley

The light that night was perfect.

Lara Swimmer

Better living through
chemistry, sans love.

Greg Rainwater

I auditioned.
I got the part.

Faith Hoffman

Entire story
    written with
        quotidian nouns.

Tim Batton

Losing your identity
can be fearsome.

Robyn Crawford

Giraffe born to a farm family.

Grant Langston

Lived life,
playing metal,
went deaf.

M. Kincaid

I write stories.
They come true.
Rebecca Woolf

Act two curtain
brought
dramatic improvements.
John Godfrey

Saw a glimpse,
should have
risked.

Lori Flaherty

Hey Red, order up! Chop! Chop!
Patty Griffin

Somehow,
she lived
without an
iPod.

Jennifer Crouser

Last words, our daughter,
   too soon.

Steve Allen

   Killed. Loved.
   Got high on everything.

David Booth

**Lonely, frothy kisses,
then only spite.**

Stephania Serena

Dead mom watching. I'll be good.

Israel Hyman

Became more like myself
   every year.

Eddie Sulimirski

Rich in degrees and student loans.

Barb Piper

He was happy being a flasher.

Fred Telegdy

Old and married.
Hot classmates. Sigh.

Bill Johnson

Nerdy, wordy, learned to shut up.

Caren Lissner

Type A personality.
Type B capability.

Keith Lang

High school dropout
but college graduate.

Mary Beth Nalin

Adolescence,
   internet, internet,
      internet, internet,
   death.

Josh Rosenfield

   We were each other's
favorite person.

Montana diLemonada

Surname rhymes with
   profanity.
      Childhood torture.

Noah Smit

   Must remember: people,
gadgets. That order.

Brian Lam

Learned to live with great loss.

Michele Wytko

Sex overrated.
Went and got castrated.

Alex Warren

Occassionally wrong but
never in doubt.

Layne Butler

Illiterate poet saw
far too much.

Robert Strassburg

WASP wants to be
soul man.

Scott Pratt

Me see world! Me write stories!

Elizabeth Gilbert

Strive, drive, arrive, alive, survive, success.

Nicholas Parsons

Normal female blogs
for a living.

Sarah Weinman

Accidents cause people
– son is wonderful.

Laurie Reinhart

Impoverished black male.
Harvard Law bound.

Robert Young

Leaving:
I toss blame like grenades.

Tanya Jarrett

Born ready, bad eyes and all.

Hua Hsu

Thought long and hard.
Got migraine.

Lisa Levy

Ten strikes against me,
hit homerun.

Maxine Jennings

Despite disorders, jafroed
jewboy gets girl.

Michael Eisner

Older orphan,
creates family with friends.

Theresa Neinas

That Kiss song says it all.

James Hampton

I can resist everything
except temptation.

Carolina Conte

Should have
risked asking, he
sighed.

Gino Serdena

Never
should've done
that first line.

Joshua MacPhetridge

Adopted?
Are you fucking
shitting me?

Darius Logan

Traveling the road,
   writing science fiction.

Henry Melton

**Hard to write poems
from prison.**

Ellen Goldstein

Born in abject obscurity;
   never escaped.

James Blum

Friends all
Jewish.
I'm merely
      neurotic.

Brian Mahon

Suburban Christian child.
Hippie agnostic adult.

Shannon Barnes

Alaskan hippie kid.
Escaped
via Ph.D.

Melanie Brewer

Clumsy girl
found adventure.
Also, bruises.

Rebecca Campbell

Jury believed me;
prison awaits him.

Jessica Yu

Realized childhood dream doesn't pay bills.

Nicole Williams

Mostly waited
for the big stuff.

Jennifer Smith

Taught lies.
Discovered truth.
Neither matters.

Gautham Nagesh

Born into a life worth living.

Cher Tushiah

Met Jesus early, then ran fast.

Jessica Thompson

I'm not afraid of anything anymore.

Kathryn Hammond

The road diverged; I took it.

Rachel Farris

Eight thousand orgasms.

Only one baby.

Neal Pollack

Loved a man, then a woman.

Kate Evans

After ages
I met my Dad.

Bryony Lee Penn

Brainy widowed sexpot
raises hell, kids.

Jennifer Johnson

Wounded girl turns
life into stories.

Farai Chideya

The militant who became a monk.

Mike Adams

Born in Baghdad,
I said enough.

Shwan Taha

Most successful accomplishments
based on spite.

Scott Birch

Haunting dad,
spotlight mom,
retrieving marriage.

Nell Casey

Blind but still saw through it.

Amanda Sibley

**Carries flask for
unsociable social events.**

Janina Williams

He wore dresses.
This caused messes.

Josh Kilmer-Purcell

Man,
slightly disgruntled,
may throw poo.

Egan Fowler

It's all about me, isn't it?

Daniel Halpern

My memoir? You can't be serious.

Dan Menaker

EDITOR. Get it?

Kate Hamill

I always took the
joke too far.

Thomas Hamill

Big nose, British chicken legs:
beautiful!

Jen Gabel

I will never be quite finished.

J. P. Hoban

Learning disability, MIT.
Never give up.

Joe Keselman

Glory developing vital loving
fighting life.

Josh Lucas

Just a rockin' readin'
knittin' kitten.

Emmeline Friedman

Looking to know everything
about everything.

Tor Andersen

**Guess my weight,
plus wheel chair.**

John Goff

Retired music teacher enjoys
life's symphonies.

Caroline Baker

Liked by all.
Known by few.

Zell Williams

Age eleven:
became a middle child.

Matt Farrell

Worse fates have befallen better men.

Stanley Morgenstern

18 years old,
   first kiss uncertainty.

Jerrica Moore

Polio gave me my happy life.

Ruth Thompson

Big heart protected
by sharp tongue.

Kris Kleindienst

I tried.
It was not
   enough.

Robert McCarty

Learned to say no too late.

Jonathan Engle

There will be no beautiful corpse.

Sharon Lewis

You must be fifty to understand.

Rev. Henri Breitenkam

Loved God, reason, simplicity; authored
books.

Patricia Williams

He always liked to live fast.

Jesse Burkett

Former child star
seeks love, employment.

Justin D. Taylor

Didn't pull out.
Downhill from there.

Roger Daubach

Fears commitment, debt.
Attracts spouse, house.

Beth Grundvig

Rubber nipples, dimpled
thumbs, Camel Lights.

Dawn Ryan

Smart, humble, shy.
Notice me, please?

Ryan Kucera

Wasn't born a redhead;
   fixed that.

Andie Grace

Found a demon to love forever.

Aaron Olson

Made costly mistakes,
learned valuable lessons.

Ricky Roach

Green eyes,
freckled skin,
waiting womb.

Heather Thompson

Naively expected logical world.
Acted foolish.

Emily Thieler

Tell your story.
That's my story.

Andy Goodman

These words are
yours to keep.

Alec Ounsworth

On the seventh
word, he rested.

Stephen J. Dubner

Index